The Disabled Child,
The Family
and
The Professional

Gloria Pollack
&
June Stewart

Whiting & Birch Ltd

MCMXCVII

© Gloria Pollack and June Stewart 1997
All rights reserved. No part of this publication may be reproduced in any form without permission. Whiting & Birch Ltd are registered with the Publishers Licensing Society, London, England and the Copyright Clearance Centre, Salem Mass. USA.

Published by Whiting & Birch Ltd,
PO Box 872, London SE23 3HL, England.
USA: Paul & Co, Publishers' Consortium Inc, PO Box 442, Concord, MA 01742.

British Library Cataloguing in Publication Data.
A CIP catalogue record is available from the British Library
ISBN 1 871177 92 8 (limp)
Printed in England by Intype, London

Contents

1. Introduction --- 1
   The role of the professional -------------------------------- 2

2. The bereavement process in parents
   of a child with disabilities --------------------------------- 4
   What is the bereavement process? --------------------------- 4
   *Why would the birth of a child with disabilities
   trigger a bereavement reaction?* ----------------------------- 5
   What feelings do parents experience? ----------------------- 6
   *What are the defences that can develop
   to alleviate certain feelings?* ------------------------------ 7
   Healing and acceptance ------------------------------------- 8
   Is there a sequence of feelings and defences? ------------- 9
   Atypical grief -- 10
   *Some advice for professionals stemming
   from the bereavement model* --------------------------------- 12

3. The process of adjustment in parents -------------------- 13
   Understanding the child's disability ---------------------- 14
   Regaining self esteem ------------------------------------- 15
   *Making sense of the event of having
   a child with disabilities* ---------------------------------- 16
   *Providing appropriate stimulation
   and handling of behaviours* --------------------------------- 17
   *Establishing healthy emotional relations
   with the child* --- 18
   Learning to manage time ----------------------------------- 20
   Learning to identify and use available resources --------- 21
   Personal growth --- 22
   *Some points about the practical use
   of the adjustment model* ------------------------------------ 23

4. A closer look at counselling — 24
    What is counselling? — 24
    Basic counselling skills — 25
    The needs of the professional — 28

5. How to work with families — 32
    The early sessions — 32
    The middle stage — 35
    Issues for the middle stage — 36
    The final stage — 44
    Issues for the final stage — 44

6. The needs of the child — 48
    Identifying needs:
       The process of diagnosis — 49
       The use of developmental charts — 50
    The debate on stimulation — 56
    Dealing with behaviour problems — 59
    Expanding the child's environment — 61

7. The use of networks to offer a whole service to disabled children and their families — 63

8. Case studies — 67

Appendices
  1. A rough guide to the Children Act 1989 for professionals working with children with disabilities — 84

  2. Code of Practice on the identification and assessment of special educational needs: A brief guideline with special references to preschool children — 89

  3. Useful books and other resources — 96

  4. Chart for a professional assessment of family adjustment to handicap — 100

Acknowledgements

To all the parents and children who have enriched our knowledge as individuals and as professionals, and to Lil Graham for her invaluable assistance with this project throughout the years.

One

Introduction

THE DIAGNOSIS of a disability in a child triggers extremely powerful feelings and defences in the family members. These feelings and defences, and the sequence in which they occur, are similar to those observed in mourning processes; in this case the loss is probably that of the expected child who would have all the attributes of normality.

Bereavement is not an illness but a normal healthy process which follows certain recognised patterns. However, every individual mourns in a different way and these differences are just as important as the similarities which can be observed.

In parallel with or following the mourning process, families with a disabled child go through a series of practical, psychological, spiritual, and social adjustments. These include aspects such as:

- understanding the disability;
- learning to provide appropriate stimulation;
- establishing a healthy relationship with the child;
- keeping or regaining a positive self image;

- using the resources available;
- and integrating the child's needs with the needs of other family members.

The process of mourning and the process of adjustment are inter-dependent in the sense that resolving the bereavement facilitates all the other adjustments. The end result is often acceptance and personal growth for parents and siblings.

The role of the professional

Professionals working with families who have a disabled child need to be aware of all these aspects so that they can understand rather than pity or criticise, so that they can hold parents in their period of grief and so that they can provide suitable advice when required. Last, but not least, they need to be able to cope with their own feelings and defences when confronted with the powerful feelings and defences of others.

For the purpose of understanding the types of interactions that occur between families and professionals, it would be useful to classify the involvement of the latter in three categories:

- Professionals who see the family *and* the child on an *occasional* basis, e.g. paediatricians, psychologists, general practitioners.
- Professionals who work *regularly* with the *child* and who interact with the *parents* only *occasionally* or *superficially*, e.g. teachers, nursery nurses, respite care workers, physiotherapists.
- Professionals *closely* involved with the *family* on a *regular* basis, e.g. health visitors, Portage workers, social workers.

It is possible of course for professionals quoted in the first two groups to take a more intensive role with the family. But in general those who belong to the third group will, and should, take the role of key workers, able to attend to the

INTRODUCTION

multiple needs of families as already described. These workers will have to be understanding of the grief process that the family goes through and be able to counsel them. They will also need to be able to guide parents in their adaptation to their new situation and empower them to cope eventually by themselves. The key worker will have to know about techniques for stimulating the child's development and managing difficult behaviour. Finally, it is also important that the professional is aware of the network of resources available in the community in order to be able to facilitate the use of all these possible resources by the family.

The professionals who see parents of disabled children only occasionally, will not need all the above knowledge all of the time. However, it is vital that they understand the full internal world of the family and that they are aware of their complex needs. Otherwise their appreciation of the child will be flawed, and they will run the risk that their advice and guidance may be inappropriate, misunderstood or simply rejected. It is absolutely impossible to attend to the disabled child's needs in isolation from those of the family.

The contents of this book are intended to introduce all professionals working in the field of child disability to the complexities of understanding and working with a family who has a child with special needs. It provides those professionals acting as key workers with the skills and knowledge that they need in order to offer families a comprehensive service. It also aims to give an insight to all those involved in the field of disability of the need to consider first and foremost the emotional world of the family. This however, should not imply any neglect of the practical needs of the child, the parents and the siblings.

Two

The bereavement process in parents of a child with disabilities

What is the bereavement process?

WHEN HUMAN beings face a severe loss, they experience very strong feelings such as shock, numbness, despair or anger. These feelings may be so intense that the person cannot cope with the pain without resorting to *defence mechanisms*. These are methods which human beings normally use to protect themselves against impulses, threats or anxiety. They include reactions such as denial, projection of anger or withdrawal.

It has been found that after the experience of loss, these feelings and defences tend to follow a certain sequence which is called the *bereavement process*.

The types of losses that can generate a bereavement process are varied and include: death of a loved one; divorce; losing one's job; exile or disability. It has long been recognised that the diagnosis of disability in a child also produces reactions akin to the bereavement process in the parents.

However, professionals should be aware of individual differences. Not all or even most parents experience all the feelings or defences, the sequence and the length of the process may vary from one person to another. Some parents may take a year to reach the acceptance or healing stage, while others never do. The intensity of feelings and their expression will vary, and the same will happen with the defence mechanisms.

Why would the birth of a child with disabilities trigger a bereavement reaction?

Even before a pregnancy occurs, human beings have a host of expectations about how a son or a daughter would be. These expectations may vary depending on many factors, but basically the anticipation is that the child that will be produced will have all the attributes of normality. Moreover, a child is an affirmation of one's success—a projection of parents into the future, who may be seen as a future companion or as somebody who will achieve things that parents did not achieve.

The disclosure of a disability in the child shatters all these anticipations, and the parents may feel that they have lost that normal child that would fulfil the expectations that they have had. Instead they look ahead and they see hardship, suffering for them and their child and no positives. They grieve the loss of their perfect child and they have to start adjusting to this loss.

What feelings do parents experience?

Numbness

When the disclosure is made to parents in cases when the abnormality of the child was unexpected, their reaction is one of numbness, an absence of feelings. They experience a loss of reality, a sense of dreaming. This type of reaction lasts from a few minutes to a few days.

Anger

This is a very common feeling after any loss. In the case of parents of children with disabilities, the anger is mainly directed towards the hospital where the child was born, the professional who made the initial diagnosis and, on rare occasions, towards the spouse or his or her family of origin. At later stages the parents may acknowledge their mixture of anger and love towards the disabled child, which in a psychotherapeutic model can be interpreted as a healthy stage, provided that the direct expression of anger does not mean harsh treatment of the child. Anger for some parents is totally justified when professionals have been dismissive, less than truthful or ignorant; or where resources important for the well-being of the child or family are not available.

Guilt

Sometimes, guilt takes the form of an irrational feeling of being punished for something the parents have done, not necessarily connected with the pregnancy or birth; as for instance, not being married to the child's father, or having committed wrong-doings in the past. More common are the mothers who blame themselves for self-neglect such as smoking during pregnancy or neglecting an illness in their child that later leads to the disability.

Sadness and despair

Sadness is frequently, but not always, expressed in crying behaviour. Often parents are congratulated for being 'brave' and this reduces the normal expression of sadness and may even inhibit the experience of those feelings. Parents may need permission to express the sadness and to see crying as a healthy behaviour. Alongside the sadness there is a feeling of despair and hopelessness, the pain will not go, life will always be unbearable, normality will never be restored. When this happens it is not helpful to offer rational arguments to counteract the parents' pain. It is better just to say that the pain is helpful and normal, and that with time it will be less frequent and intense.

What are the defences that can develop to alleviate certain feelings?

Denial

This is a very common feature in the bereavement process and it can be expressed in many different ways. Parents frequently deny the severity or even the existence of their child's disability. The parent of a Down's Syndrome child may say how 'normal' she looks and may even query if there may be a mistake. In the case of children with no genetic or physical damage, the process of denial is even more pronounced. Very often parents will stress that 'there is nothing wrong with the child except for a speech problem' and that everything would be fine once the child can talk. Some parents accept the here and now of the disability but cling for a long time to the idea of a 'normal' future, or even a magical cure.

Projection

Projection as a defence means that feelings that are really directed towards somebody are instead felt towards another person. In the case of parents of children with disabilities their feelings of anger tend to be projected frequently, but not always, towards people outside their family. This is expressed by attributing blame to the hospital or doctor who delivered the child, or to the general practitioner who did not refer the child soon enough, to the social worker who is unhelpful or to the teacher who is not obtaining good results from the child. These complaints can be justified and then they are not projections, but often the person receiving hostile feelings is only a convenient recipient of the parent's anger. It is important in these cases that the professional should get support to understand the mechanisms leading to the rejection. This will help them to cope better and be more tolerant towards the parents and less critical towards themselves.

Repression

This is the mechanism through which unacceptable or threatening experiences are kept unconscious. Parents who use this type of defence will reject their feelings following the disclosure of disability or will say that they only lasted a few days. They may say that their disabled son or daughter makes no difference and is the same as their other normal children. They will not acknowledge ever experiencing pain or anger.

Withdrawal

Parents who are very anxious or in too much pain will avoid any reminders of their child's difficulties. They may not attend meetings about their child, may avoid meeting parents of normal children or will fail appointments to psychologists, paediatricians or other professionals who will talk about the disability or who may give an 'official' diagnosis.

Healing and acceptance

After a period of approximately one to three years or even longer the healing process can be clearly observed. Having worked through the pain and the denial, the parents regain, or even gain for the first time a sense of well-being. It is not a time which is free of anxiety, sadness or even crisis periods, but the pain is less raw, opinions are more based on reality and they have come to a point when they fully accept the child just as what s/he is. As one mother pointed out 'I do not want her different. If she could run and talk she would not be her'.

Is there a sequence of feelings and defences?

In common with other bereavement processes, mourning for parents of children with disabilities tend to follow certain stages. Different authors have given different labels to these stages and there are some variations in the different models. There are also individual variations when some stages are reversed or omitted, and as it will be seen in the next section there are cases where the process does not develop or does not even start.

There are also 'crisis periods' when after the healing has occurred the whole process seems to start again. A new diagnosis, starting school, leaving school, or a deterioration of the child can be extremely upsetting, but these second crises tend to be shorter and more bearable if the first process has been fully accomplished.

The sequence after bereavement most commonly described goes through the following stages:

1. shock and numbness;
2. denial, often interspersed with anger and guilt;
3. sadness and despair;
4. healing.

Atypical grief

As in all cases of bereavement, there are sometimes instances of atypical grief expressed through prolonged denial or displacement of feelings. This reaction to grief can be linked to life experiences pre-dating the birth of the disabled child, unresolved situations of the past that interfere with the progress of the bereavement process. Atypical grief leads to chronic maladaptive reactions that can take various forms.

Persistent denial

Very few parents will deny the child's disability for ever, even though some will search years for a professional who will say that the early diagnosis was erroneous. But then, when the diagnosis is fully accepted the parents will continue shopping around, this time in search of a miracle cure. Parents like these are very vulnerable to charlatans or money-making professionals.

Continuous rage

The anger that the child with a disability triggers will not go away in certain cases. Parents of adolescent children will be dissatisfied with every teacher, every doctor and every person, professional or not, who tries to help them. This behaviour sometimes goes together with the 'search for a miracle cure' and each professional is rejected angrily when they don't fulfil the parents' expectations.

The feelings that the parent may have about not being a 'good enough' parent, or of not having a 'good enough' child, are constantly projected onto outsiders who can never be good enough.

Chronic over-involvement

Constant activity is a way to keep pain at an unconscious level. The parent who stimulates the child constantly, who is always kept busy by activities related to the child is basically trying not to experience the pain or perhaps the guilt that the child brings.

Rejection and compensation

Rejection expressed in neglect or excessive chastisement is easily identified by professionals who will then try to offer alternative care on a full or part time basis. A more subtle situation is that of a parent who compensates for his or her true feelings of rejection by excessive possessiveness and over-protection. Most of the time the parent is not aware of the real feelings behind the excessive concern and it is very difficult for professionals to modify this attitude which in the long run is damaging for the child.

In all the above cases the family, as a unit, is negatively affected, but because of the deep rooted nature of the problem, rational discussions with the parents yield no positive results. Sometimes a discussion at an early stage of previous traumatic experiences may help to open up the defences, but in most cases psychotherapeutic intervention for the parents is the best alternative. Alas! this is seldom accepted.

Some advice for professionals stemming from the bereavement model

- Professionals who work with children with disabilities have to be aware of the powerful feelings that the parents are experiencing and the defences that they may develop.
- These feelings and defences, no matter how irrational they may appear to the professional, are a healthy reaction to a traumatic event. They can not and should not be counteracted using rational arguments or authoritarian advice.
- Professionals who have regular involvement with parents should support them in working through their feelings. Counselling techniques are needed for this work.
- While the bereavement process goes on, parents may or may not feel able to engage in certain activities such as working intensely with the child, not being over-protective, attending meetings or appointments. Professionals should not judge or criticize and should not overload the parents with requests before they are ready to accept them.
- Defence mechanisms are built to hide from the person and from others, events or feelings which are too painful. The professional should try to understand this hidden meaning but not force the interpretation onto the parent.
- It is important to be aware of the concept of projected anger and try not to be too upset or too angry when one is the recipient of the parents' hostility.
- As with all clients, parents of children with disabilities need to develop trust with professionals. Therefore they need to be treated with honesty, respect and sympathy.
- The key worker should consult and if necessary refer to a qualified counsellor, if the grief, anger or denial that parents are experiencing does not show signs of diminishing.

Three

The process of adjustment in parents

TO INTEGRATE a child with disabilities in a family and to help develop his or her full potential, the parents must make psychological, practical and social adjustments which are far greater than those required after the birth of a normal child.

Moreover, the strong feelings and defences which were described in the previous section can interfere with the adjustment tasks, and often these will be achieved only after the resolution of the bereavement process.

Susan Le Poidevin, a woman who became blind as the result of an accident in adulthood, developed a model of adjustment to loss in the case of disability that is also appropriate as a frame of reference to describe the experiences of parents of a disabled child.

The following is a description of the tasks to be encountered in this process of adjustment as described in Le Poidevin's model.

First Task:
Understanding the child's disability

This relates to the parents' ability to accept the diagnosis and the implication for the present and the future. It also means accepting the uncertainties, even the fact that a diagnostic label may never be available. This part of the adjustment means that parents will already be working successfully through the process of denial.

How can the professional help?

- Handing over leaflets, booklets or books describing the child's condition.
- Sharing with parents the information available from other professionals, or more likely helping them to interpret, understand and integrate information that the parents have already been given about their child.
- Giving addresses of parents of children with similar problems (of course if they are agreeable) or of societies that specialise in the particular disability.

It has to be remembered that at certain stages it may be painful for parents to receive this information and that their wishes should always be respected.

Second Task:
Regaining self esteem

The goal here is to work towards a satisfactory identity and self concept for the child and the family. This means that they should not feel inferior, ashamed or helpless about having a child with a disability. Problems in this area can for example lead to parents never taking their child outside the house, not mentioning the disability to work colleagues or not wanting to mix with parents who do not have a disabled child. It has to do with feelings of shame and envy and it is often exacerbated by a society which rejects disability. For instance, siblings often suffer feelings of inferiority provoked by taunting remarks made by their peers with respect to their brother or sister who has a disability. Sometimes parents may observe neighbours crossing the road when they see them walking with their child.

How can the professional help?

What parents need most is to be valued and for their child to be valued as well. The attitudes of the professionals that they encounter is therefore of great importance. They need to be treated as people who are many other things apart from being parents of a disabled child. Their personal skills and qualities should be acknowledged and encouraged. Sometimes parents' groups can be very useful to build self esteem but not everybody wishes to belong to groups.

Third Task:
Making sense of the event of having a child with disabilities

This refers mainly to the question 'Why me?' and all the issues that this raises: the person's belief system, fate, faith and view of life. Parents work through this issue in many different ways, some probably not considering it at all. Some parents lose faith; for others their faith is strengthened; some see the event as a punishment, others as the will of God who has chosen them. This is not necessarily a religious issue; it is also an existential philosophical question that can be resolved without reference to religious faith.

How can the professional help?

The role of the professional here is mainly that of a good listener who facilitates adjustment within the parents' values and never imposes his or her own views on the purpose or meaning of life. Techniques such as rephrasing, integrating the parents' observations, or reminding them of previous comments, can be useful as well as general non-directive questions.

Fourth Task:
Providing appropriate stimulation and handling of behaviour

Children with disabilities usually have special needs. They may benefit from specific teaching of language skills or may require physiotherapy. They may need to be fed for a long time or they may be using a tube to be fed. The practical demands may be to manage difficult behaviour appropriately or provide enriching experiences at the right level of development. To accomplish these tasks often parents need practical help, other people who will share the teaching and stimulation of the child and specialists who offer treatment, advice or equipment.

How can professionals help?

Professionals should be able to offer programmes, advice and equipment. These programmes and advice should be appropriate to the child's needs and the parents' needs. Sometimes parents want very structured programmes, sometimes they prefer general advice. Some parents just need reassurance that they are doing their best. Parents often feel less pressurised and less guilty if the teaching and handling of behaviour is shared with teachers or nursery nurses. Professionals working with parents should know about these facilities and how to accede to them.

Fifth Task:
Establishing healthy emotional relations with the child

This task is related to the healing stage in the bereavement process which implies a full and realistic acceptance of the child. The focus here is to establish a healthy relationship between the parents, the siblings and the child, which is sometimes difficult to achieve, given the feelings and defences that the child has generated.

Fulfilling this task means achieving the expression of warmth and anger; that is, not being afraid to show negative feelings towards the child and also allowing siblings to express their anger. It also means accepting the child's limitations and acknowledging strengths and potentials. A balance then will be achieved and there will be neither overprotection or excessive demands. Some parents who have not adjusted in this area have either too little expectations and give not enough stimulation, or they are never satisfied with the child's progress.

All these positive adjustments mean that the child will have a positive self image as projected by the other members of the family.

How can professionals help?

There are two main things that parents need to make this adjustment, the first is to be given permission to express all their feelings toward the child and the resulting experiences that have been generated. The second is to feel that others value their child in a realistic way. Professionals should not discourage parents' expression of anger or desperation. If they say that they can't stand the child, that it's driving them crazy, they should not be criticised and their feelings should be validated. Saying 'It must be difficult for you', 'Some times children can be nerve racking', is a way to accept the parents' feelings. The feelings of jealousy or anger in siblings also need validating, after all very few people will be unaware that brothers and sisters call each other names or fight even when there is no question of disability involved.

In terms of the second need, that is, valuing the child, professionals should not collude with parents' defences when they say nothing is wrong, but they should always try to find areas of progress, to praise and celebrate the child. They should, in general, convey to parents the uniqueness and the value of their son or daughter.

Sixth Task:
Learning to manage time

The excessive demands put on parents after the birth or diagnosis of a child with disabilities mean that they have little time for the other children, for their spouses or for themselves as individuals. It is essential to adjust to this disequilibrium and to restore normality to all the family of which the child is a member with no more and no less rights than the others. This may be one of the most difficult tasks to achieve because it means that, contrary to normal expectations, the mother, in order to survive, cannot be the only care-giver. In the most successful cases, the father is incorporated into the 'team', sharing responsibilities, and the parents can also entrust their child to someone outside the family unit through respite schemes, family centres or nurseries. The resulting adjustment will mean that the child's needs are attended to and so are the needs of the other family members.

How can professionals help?

The child's needs are often so great that there is little time for the parents, particularly the mothers to attend to anything else. But it is also common that out of guilt, parents do not give themselves permission to lead a more independent and enriching life; the guilt may even be forced onto the other children who have to accept that they always come second to their disabled brother or sister. Parents may reject all type of outside respite because of this feeling of guilt and become 'martyrs' on behalf of their child. If the guilt generated during the bereavement process is dealt with successfully, then the professional will be able to encourage the use of outside resources, the development of parents as individuals and the attendance to the needs of the other children. Sometimes, the scarcity of resources prevents the attainment of this task and parents are forced into conditions which mean that their psychological well being is badly affected.

Seventh Task:
Learning to identify
and use available resources

If the parents have developed an acceptance of the situation, they should also, with guidance, have acquired a grasp of the resources available - school, respite, allowances. To achieve optimum quality of life they need to learn how the different agencies operate as a system. This system can be difficult to negotiate and parents may face bureaucratic red tape, insufficient resources, or unhelpful officers or professionals. Therefore, parents will need to develop assertiveness skills. It is of common occurrence to find parents who are naturally timid and quiet and that, in a positive reaction, become much more confident and outspoken. They learn to negotiate without aggression and not to feel shame or guilt when requiring support for their child or their family.

How can professionals help?

It is important for professionals to be aware of the facilities, resources and benefits which are available, and to guide parents appropriately. They also need to be supportive to parents who are negotiating the system. Initially, and particularly during the bereavement period, the professionals may need to do the negotiating on behalf of the parents. During later stages they should encourage them to learn to identify and obtain resources for themselves.

Eighth Task:
Personal growth

As often happens with the experiences of big crisis situations, the end product may be personal growth. The parents who have worked through these various adjustments may reach a stage where they can look at wider issues that may or may not be related to disability. They may have moved from despair to self confidence. Successfully resolving the crisis gives them more insight into their lives. Couples may re-negotiate their marriage, parents may feel confident to pursue further education or they may work for better facilities for the disabled either individually or in groups. This task is not part of the process of readjustment and is not necessary for a return to a state of equilibrium. But it is a by product that professionals observe with pride and hope, in their work with parents of children with disability.

Some points about the practical use of the adjustment model

- The adjustment model is not a 'stages' model. The various tasks do not follow a predetermined sequence and achieving one task is not a pre-requisite to embark in another one.
- The professional who uses this model when supporting parents, will find it useful to fill in the charts that accompany this book (see Appendix 4). They will provide a guide and a reminder of the tasks that parents have achieved and those that they are dealing or about to deal with.
- The use of the model, facilitated by the chart, helps the professional to conceptualise the picture of the whole family. Having all these dimensions to consider is useful to balance strengths with problem areas which should be explored, and if necessary, become the focus of advice, practical help or counselling.

Four

A closer look at counselling

ALTHOUGH THIS book is not intended to offer counselling training as such, its approach does emphasise the need for a basic understanding of the use of a professional relationship at the core of working with families who are caring for a child with disabilities.

What is counselling?

Counselling is a widely used, and sometimes abused term. It therefore, appears necessary to determine what counselling is, in a professional sense. It is sometimes useful to approach a definition by a process of exclusion. In essence, counselling is not the giving of information, though information may be given in counselling. Neither is the giving of advice, recommendations and suggestions, although counselling is often camouflaged as such. Counselling is not about directly influencing attitudes, beliefs or behaviour by means of persuading, leading or convincing, no matter how subtly.

A CLOSER LOOK AT COUNSELLING

What then is counselling? Counselling is concerned with the reduction of conflict, a healing process leading to personal growth, which often does result in changes in behaviour, but at the client's pace and following his or her agenda. The counselling relationship is one in which an atmosphere is created in which the individual is able to take responsibility for him or herself, and to begin to develop, or to restore the self-esteem which is necessary for his or her functioning as a healthy, responsible, independent human being. Primarily, this helpful atmosphere is more dependent upon the attitudes and feelings of the counsellor towards the client than upon the technique she uses.

Basic counselling skills

Having said that the counsellor's feelings and attitudes towards the client are paramount, there are certain core requirements for counselling. These are outlined below and particular reference is made to the extra issues of bereavement and disability.

1. Listening with the 'third ear'

If the professional is concerned about empowering parents and hence facilitating the healthy development of all the children in the family s/he must listen attentively to the expressed feelings whilst being aware that, below the surface, there are deeper issues to be addressed. The over-riding issue is that of parental grief, and this is often the trigger for the emergence of other conflicts. To this end, time must be allowed in the sessions for the expression of feelings, and for the exploration of these feelings.

2. The unconditional acceptance of the client family

This calls into question the professional's basic philosophy towards other people. The client must be treated as a worthy person; being respected by another is the first step in achieving self-respect. The counsellor accepts the child as s/he is, without judgement, condemnation, criticism or ridicule. This is most obviously pertinent in the field of disability, as children with special needs can be born into all socio-economic groups. Furthermore, as 'acceptance' is a major issue in coming to terms with the child's problems, it is vital that the parents, in their turn, also feel accepted.

3. Start where the client is at

This is a counselling cliche' which should not be forgotten. The professional must pitch his/her approach at the client's level of personal development, with particular attention paid to where they are in the bereavement process, e.g. if the parents are still very deeply in the phase of anger then the professional has to stay with the anger until they are ready to feel the real sorrow.

4. Awareness of the client's uniqueness

The allowance of individual differences is essential, being mindful of the uniqueness of individuals and families. This is a pre-requisite for all counselling work, and is no less important in families where there is disability and the accompanying grief reactions. One may be able to map out a normal grief process, but each individual makes the journey through that process in his/her own style.

5. Making a commitment

It is also very important to recognise that the bereavement process can take two to three years to run its course under normal circumstances. It therefore must be accepted that there is a long term commitment to the family. It can be a number of years before the diagnosis for a child is clear, and the family will need help during these uncertain times. This commitment need not take the form of weekly visits, but the clients need to know that the professional will be in regular contact over many months.

6. Patience is essential

This is clearly linked to skill (5) and the bereavement process. Let the client dictate the pace. This is perhaps one of the hardest stances to maintain when, as a professional, you can see the issues quite clearly and feel that you know what is in the clients' best interest, while they are still resistant.

7. Be reliable

Reliability is critical; try never to fail an appointment without good cause. Because of the birth of the child with a disability, some clients may already have a fragile sense of worth, and failed appointments may signal to them that they are not worthy of professional attention, or are too difficult to help. More importantly, though, feelings and topics for discussion may well have been made ready for discussion in preparation for the visit. It can be upsetting or even damaging if the parents are deprived of the promised outlet at the last minute.

8. Develop a consistency of approach

As the world inhabited by the families of children with disabilities is full of uncertainties, it is very helpful for them to know where they stand with regard to at least one professional who has a consistent model of working. Consistency, however, must not be confused with inflexibility, bearing in mind some of the other core skills.

9. Be aware of your own agenda

It is important that the professional knows himself/herself and his own sore points, so that the clients' already complex world is not further complicated by the counsellor's own agenda or unresolved issues. e.g. it could be very unhelpful if a professional has his/her own unworked through griefs. This point is particularly worth considering when looking at the possibility of parents counselling other parents. Broadly speaking, both professionals and parents helpers are most useful to clients when they have worked through their own painful agendas

In addition, professionals should guard against entering into 'competition' with parents. Parents will always be more important to the child than professionals and in most cases, are the most powerful influence in helping the child's whole development and personal growth. If the alliance between parents and professionals is not based on mutuality the professional can find herself partially or completely 'blocked' in her efforts to help.

It will be noted that no techniques for achieving rapport with clients have been described; such techniques are neither necessary nor desirable. They are usually about the insecurity of the counsellor rather than about the needs of the client. Rapport is not something to be achieved by artificial methods or social devices. It is something that develops and exists where the counsellor is genuinely interested in the client and his/her problems. The development of the basic skills and attitudes described above should facilitate the establishment of rapport. The expression of these skills must be genuine and spontaneous, not laboured or self-conscious. Don't be afraid of bringing your own style and self to the work.

The needs of the professional

So far consideration has been given to the parents' feelings and attitudes and how the professional can be tuned in to these to benefit children with disabilities and their families. What then of the professional's feelings about him or herself towards the client?

There is a whole army of feelings that a professional might have about his/her client; and not all positive. For example:

Anger

at the attitude of some parents towards their children, or on the behalf of parents who have been mishandled by the system.

Frustration

at the parents' inability to use help, or to use it quickly enough.

Sorrow

at the plight of some children and their families and the apparent hopelessness of their situation.

Inadequacy

in the face of such grief, and seemingly insoluble problems. This is particularly difficult for professionals who are used to being able to solve their clients' difficulties and make things better.

Dislike

of some parents who may direct their anger and disappointment at the professional and increase his/her feelings of inadequacy.

Guilt

Professionals may particularly feel guilt about these negative feelings towards his/her clients and regret that they have failed to 'rise above' these feelings. Additionally, in some cases there may be guilt feelings about the relief felt that this is not happening to them; a sort of 'guilt of the survivor' response.

Attachment

It is also very common for professionals to have great feelings of affection and admiration towards the child with the disability and the family caring for him. There are positive facets to this in that families can feel that their less than perfect child may be unlovable, or that they themselves have become marginalised, and a professional who accepts and cares for them can offer a healing experiencing. However, this can lead to over-identification with the family, and subsequently the professional may collude with the denial process or the inappropriate projections of anger onto other professionals or institutions. This could impair the family's growth.

If not properly checked, feelings can cloud the relationship with the family, however, it is important to remember two things. Firstly, if professionals were not moved by the behaviour, suffering, and plight of others, the helping professions would be seriously lacking. Secondly, and very importantly, professionals should not be afraid of, nor ashamed of, their own feelings, particularly as a lot can be learned from them. Provided the professional is in a reasonably good mood, not too distracted by personal problems, nor too pressurised, then the feelings about the client can be very instructive.

For example, the professional's own spontaneous feelings and emotions, as they tune into the client, may provide the key for understanding behaviours or attitudes to the client which are at first incomprehensible. The parents will be feeling more hurt and threatened than the professionals, and possibly more cut off from their true emotions. The professional should have a more developed capacity to tolerate conflict and anxiety, and by putting themselves 'into the other's shoes', they can perhaps allow themselves to feel what the client has been unable to acknowledge in himself/herself. Hence, feeling moved to tears in the presence of a parent who has not yet cried, may indicate a tapping into that parent's unshed tears. Or if you are feeling inadequate in the face of tremendous grief, this may be a measure of the client's feelings of inadequacy. The key to making sense of this is knowing what is your own emotional material and what belongs to the client.

Another key element in the client/professional relationship is the awareness of the feelings a client may impose or project upon the professional. These may or may not be warranted, but the professional may be treated to anger or rejection really meant for somebody else, or conversely, the client may be inappropriately waiting for rejection or criticism because this is what has come to be expected from 'authority figures'.

It is not unusual for the professional to feel wholly positive about the family with whom s/he is working; to feel admiration and affection. It is equally important to remember personal boundaries in these situations as it is in the more conflict-laden cases. The professional's desire to make right a child's problems can lead to false reassurance and collusion with the parents which will inevitably invoke bad feelings in the worker.

Clearly, all these factors can take their toll on the professional working in this field, and it is essential that they make time and space to share experiences with peers. To summarise, professionals working in this field need to:

1. Get supervision and support from peers.
2. Be able to discriminate their own agenda from that of the client.
3. Learn to tolerate and accept their own feelings, even negative ones.
4. Use their feelings to further understanding of their clients and indeed themselves.
5. Spot projections and not automatically take them at face value.

Five

How to work with families

The early sessions

STARTING TO work with a new family and their unique set of circumstances can be daunting. The first tasks are threefold:

1. To allow the parents to tell their story, including practical details about their child's condition.
2. To describe the professional's role and set out a framework for helping.
3. To begin to establish a relationship with one or more members of the family.

1. Areas for initial investigation

To address these three tasks can take a number of visits, but allowing the parent to tell the story of the child's birth or diagnosis is an important facet of this stage. It is vital to know a number of things:

- About any fears during the pregnancy, or details of birth

trauma, as this may give clues about possible issues which could affect bonding with the child.
- Another important question to ask is 'How and when were you told about the child's problems?' This will set the tone for the long path towards acceptance, e.g. the mother may have had worries about the child's development for many months before diagnosis, but her fears may not have been heard or she may even have been labelled an over-anxious mother. She and the child may already be in an enmeshed relationship. Alternatively, the birth of a baby with an obvious syndrome may be dealt with so unhelpfully that the child is experienced in a wholly negative light.
- It is essential to know if the parent has cried or expressed grief in any way. This gives clues as to how s/he is functioning in the framework of the bereavement process. Time must be given for the full expression of feelings in the session; it is important that the parent feels that the professional can cope with this outpouring of grief. This experience can help the client in two ways; firstly if the professional can cope or not be destroyed by the grief, then it gives the client hope that she can cope too. Secondly, it reinforces the feeling that it is O.K. to cry; indeed this expression of grief is a necessary stepping stone in the bereavement process.
- It is useful in general to ask about the feelings around in the extended family in relation to the child. For example, it is important to know if the parents attempt to apportion blame to each other, or if grandparents attempt to deny disability in the child.
- Find out about the child's condition, and if any other key professionals are involved in his/her care. It is also useful to try to assess parental attitudes towards these professionals e.g. do they feel trust in their judgement, or are certain professionals scapegoated. This may give

indications as to how they will relate to you.
- Start to build up a picture of other helpful networks which can perhaps be integrated into your approach e.g. a grandparent who is very accepting of the child can be very validating, or a health visitor who is very sensitive to the parents' feelings can emphasise the need for expression of feelings whilst giving practical support with the baby.

2. Discussing the professional's role

Simultaneously, in these early sessions the professional is setting the scene for the work to be done in a variety of ways:

- Giving the parents a full description of the professional's role and the wider agency, and outlining the service on offer.
- Making an informal contract with the family and setting boundaries for the working relationship. e.g. How often visits will be made, the duration of the visits and indeed the possible duration of the whole period of intervention. Also, emphasise the flexible nature of the approach, the agenda being set by the client.
- Discussing confidentiality and the limits of expertise. It is useful to be able to say, for example, 'If I cannot answer your question I will say so, but I will find out or seek out someone else who can give you an answer'.
- Engaging as many family members as possible; don't focus on the mother, or worse, solely on the disabled child. It is worth noting that it is notoriously difficult to engage fathers, but well worth the effort if you can. Siblings, too, may be struggling at this time and the professional must be aware at least of their needs even at this early stage.

3. Establishing the relationship

If all goes well, within three or four sessions, the relationship with the family should be becoming established. However, a word of warning: there will always be cases where trust is slow to build or the hurt is so great the beginning stage can cover many sessions and patience is essential. Indeed, there will be a small minority of families who will not respond at all and then alternative methods of helping must be considered, e.g. enlisting the help of a trusted health visitor, or encouraging the mother to use pre-school nursery facilities and the support of specialist teachers.

The middle stage

This is usually the longest period of involvement in a relationship that can last a year or more. The family begins to trust enough to work through some of the bereavement and other issues:

- The effects of the child with the disability upon the family.
- Once they are comfortable with the words 'disability', 'handicap', 'special needs' etc, they may well want to discuss all sorts of practical problems relating to schools, benefits, respite, the child's future and so on. They may also want to begin stimulating their child using programmes at home, or sharing the task with Portage workers or other pre-school resources.
- There may even be problems related to the child's behaviour management, e.g. sleep problems, or tantrums.

Consequently, the professional's job will be to combine counselling with a task-centred approach: A whole approach for the whole family.

Issues for the middle stage

1. Working with feelings

Often there is a good deal of working through of feelings, with a lot of emphasis on sorrow in this stage. It is reassuring to be able to say to parents who are grieving normally 'This takes a long time, you may think you are going mad but you're not, eventually the pain will ease and the periods of acceptance increase'. Some part of every session should be given over to discussion of feelings; even if sometimes the parent is reluctant to express feelings, at least they know the space is there if they want it.

2. Focus on fathers

Many fathers will avoid contact with the professional, and it has been identified that their process of bereavement and adjustment to the birth of their child will be at a slower pace because they receive their help vicariously through the mother. If the father can be engaged, he is most often a source of great help and support, and he, in turn, gains in insight and personal growth.

The world of the child with a disability can be very female dominated, and this can be off putting for a potentially involved father; care must be taken to hear what he is saying during sessions or indeed take note of what he doesn't say. He can be expressing pain in other ways and it is important that he knows that he has a voice too. Of course, all this is seen in the context of a society where it is not O.K. for men to show feelings openly or express vulnerability in any way.

Fathers commonly experience one or more of the following feelings:

- He may feel 'less of a man' because he had 'produced' this less than perfect child. Sadly, there is still a belief around that men impregnate women, therefore, they are responsible for the 'quality' of the child.

If the professional gets the opportunity, and this is a big 'if' with this type of father, it would be important to talk through the often random nature of disability and try to relieve him of the feelings of responsibility.

- The father may feel ousted from his position of prime importance in the household; suddenly all the focus is on the needs of the child with the disability. He may feel that he has 'lost' his wife, as well as the imagined child, as she struggles to cope with the baby's needs.

If the professional is mindful of this possibility, the problem can be addressed carefully when helping the couple express their feelings of loss, and in helping the mother towards making appropriate boundaries with their child.

- Mothers often grow in strength with the experience of rearing a child with a disability. She may take on new and different roles and benefit from possible contact with professionals who affirm her. This can be very threatening for her partner who may feel he is diminishing in strength as his wife grows.

It is important that the professional recognises this and, given the opportunity, tries to redress the balance, emphasising the parents as partners.

- After rearing any child, men are often faced with the task of 'reclaiming' their partners and re-establishing themselves as a couple. Clearly, fathers of children with disabilities, especially in severe cases, may feel that their partners can never be reclaimed in the face of the child's extreme dependency.

This can cause feelings of disappointment and hopelessness in fathers and, if possible, the professional can try to reframe the future for the couple; recognising their needs as grown-up human beings separate from their child and emphasising a working towards independence for the child in some form, however limited.

3. Addressing the needs of siblings

Similarly, meeting the siblings of the child with a disability, and observing how they behave and function within the family, is an important part of building up a whole picture. It is well within the remit of the professional to involve siblings in discussion of their disabled brother or sister, and give them permission to have feelings too. Sometimes children's feelings are overlooked in the midst of grief, this is especially true when a child with a disability arrives into a family and the parents may be absorbed in their own coming to terms with feelings and with the new child's needs.

Children of course, will usually take their cues from parental reactions to the situation. If the parents can freely discuss ambivalent feelings towards the child with a disability, then the way is open for the children in the family to do the same.

Some issues for siblings

- *Guilt*
  The brother or sister may well have wished the disabled child ill or even dead. This can be catastrophic if the latter happens. It is important that the professional is aware of this possibility and gives a voice to these fears, stressing their normality. When unconscious issues are made conscious, they are immediately less threatening and more manageable.

- *Jealousy*
  Of necessity, when a child is born with a disability s/he will receive enormous attention from parents, other family members and numerous professionals. There will be appointments to be kept and tasks to be attended to. In the midst of all this, other children in the family will feel sold short, excluded, or even abandoned. In some cases these feelings may be based on fact.

  The professional should be mindful of this and work with the parents to redress the balance. It should be emphasised that sibling jealousy is normal with the advent of a new baby, but that these feelings are magnified when that child is so needy, and brings so many problems to the family. The sibling and the parents should be aware that it is not 'naughty', 'wicked' nor 'selfish' for the able-bodied children to want their share of parenting and family time. It is the professional's task to facilitate the parents in seeing the child with a disability as only one member of the family unit.

- *Damaged self-image*
  Indeed the whole family will suffer from this in the early stages of adjusting to the birth of their special needs child. This will be the first dent in the self-image of the sibling who will again be influenced by the reactions of his parents. Depending on the age and stage in development of the healthy sibling, self-image can be affected in different ways, e.g. a toddler may feel his role really usurped, and that he lacks importance to his parents and other adults, while an adolescent whose sense of self is in turmoil already may experience a sense of embarrassment or shame which may deeply affect confidence.

  As the professional works with the family, s/he will be hopefully enhancing the members sense of being valued and worthwhile. Siblings should be involved in this process, encouraged to enjoy the child with the disability, and be rewarded and valued for his or her contribution to the family unit. However, it is important that siblings should never be seen merely as extra helpers for the disabled child. The family's and the siblings' own strengths and normality should be stressed at every opportunity. The sibling should be seen as a separate, whole person not as an appendage to the disabled brother or sister, nor indeed should the able bodied child be expected to compensate for that sibling by achieving extra accolades educationally or socially.

- *Bullying and other external factors*
  These children are living in a world that is prejudiced in many ways, not least of all towards disability. Bullying is now recognised as a terrible hazard for some children, and those who have a disabled member in their family could fall prey to this. Even mild 'skitting' or name-calling can cause pain to a child or young person who is already struggling with a multitude of other feelings. In their efforts to protect their already worried parents from further anxiety, children may keep these painful experiences to themselves.

  Those professionals working with families can open up this possibility in a matter of fact way by merely making the statement 'some children with disabled brothers or sisters get skitted'. This may allow even a general discussion of the issue which may be helpful for the sibling in distress. Hopefully, as the child grows in confidence, s/he will find his or her own coping mechanisms.

- *Fears for the future*
  It is not unusual for the older siblings of children with

disabilities to already be afraid of what their responsibilities might be when their parents can no longer take care of the disabled child. Furthermore, these older siblings may also be concerned about their own vulnerability to bearing a child with disabilities.

It is very important that the professional reduces the taboo in the family about these painful issues and tries to promote sensitive open discussion. At the very least the parents should be made aware that their other children are experiencing these fears and should be given confidence to answer any questions about the child's condition in an open manner.

If any of these issues becomes too handicapping for the child who has a brother or sister with a disability, then it may be advisable to get individual help for him or her -e.g. through play therapy or counselling, or the involvement of teachers with school-related problems. In some areas of the country there are organized groups of siblings of disabled children which could be beneficial to enhance self esteem and discuss special problems.

4. Problems with family relationships

Some of the family history may begin to unfold, and marital discord or family estrangements may be exposed. It is useful for the professional to allow for this in the sessions, to reassure parents that s/he is interested in the whole family's well-being and that these issues are important. It is not usually helpful to give direct advice about personal relationships, but it is useful to acknowledge the pain that such conflict is causing. Sometimes, some of this conflict can be normalised and put in perspective in the light of the trauma, other times the relationship problems may be deeper rooted. In the latter case there may be room for further exploration as the parent begins to get stronger and look towards personal development. This may not happen until the end of the middle phase, or even in the end stage.

Sometimes, this sort of disclosure can provide a warning that work with a particular family will not be easy or straight forward. If the conflict pre-dates the birth of the child with a disability the prognosis may not be good for the resolution of the relationship problems, or problems of individual pathology. The client might either resist change to the extent that s/he focuses entirely on the disabled child as a diversion from deeper problems, or if personal change takes place, marriages may end or other family relationships may permanently alter.

In these circumstances, the professional involved with the family is not there to take sides but to listen and support and, if appropriate get the family some specialist help e.g. Marital Therapy or Family Therapy

5. Helping with practical issues

- There may well have been a good deal of focus on the needs of the child with the disability in this middle stage. There may be behaviour management problems with which parents will need guidance and support and it will often be appropriate to help to stimulate the child within the home to work alongside other professionals in ensuring the child's proper development.
- The parents are beginning to accept the problems both of the 'here and now' and for the future. There will be questions to be answered, or at least issues to be discussed openly; possibly about education or independent living in the future. Helping the parents to live with the unknown is very important; it can be useful to say 'Nobody knows what the future holds for our child, not even the so-called experts - they find it hard living with not having the answers too. In fact no-one really knows what the future

holds for any of us'.

- Hand in hand with this it is important to regularly focus on the child's progress, give help with strengths and weaknesses in the child's development. It is helpful too, to discuss respite care and sharing the child's care with a view to enhancing independence and quality of life for the child with the disability and other family members.
- By the end of this middle stage, the professional's work may have already involved him or her in liaising with other agencies and resources. Part of the professional's role is to be aware of the task of helping to meet the practical needs of the family as an aid to its members in working through the bereavement and adjustment process. In the early stages of acceptance, the parents may still be so grief-stricken that the professional has to organise resources on their behalf. S/he must be aware, however, that the skill is in knowing when to withdraw this type of support and facilitate the parents to do their own negotiating for resources.

There is always the dilemma of when to 'hold' and when to 'push' the client and generally speaking, by this stage, the parents are well able to give you the right messages, and the professional usually hears those messages correctly. Furthermore, by this stage, the professional will have, in effect, 'modelled' how to deal with Housing Departments, or grant-making organisations by sharing copies of letters or the content of telephone conversations with the parents. It is always a good idea to share tasks with the parents e.g. 'I'll set up the visit to the nursery class, if you keep the appointment yourselves'. Latterly, it is always a pleasant surprise to hear from the parents that they have taken it upon themselves to sort out a difficulty, and often found a satisfactory solution. The professional then knows s/he can let go of this role with the parents.

The final stage

Working with endings is a hard won skill. Often, after an association of up to two years, through 'thick and thin', both parents and professionals can be very reluctant to end the contact. However, this can be a very therapeutic period in the relationship. There are certain tasks to be addressed:

- Reviewing achievements and charting progress, ensuring that the bereavement and adjustment processes have largely been worked through, reminding the parents that whilst some of these feelings may come again in the face of future crisis, families now have the insight and the mechanisms to help them to cope.
- Checking that the family and the child have had their practical needs met as far as possible.
- Perhaps working on new goals with the family, e.g. mother maybe looking at returning to work or further education., the marital couple may be planning to have more time to themselves.
- The actual closing of the case can signal a return to normality, a new equilibrium and this is to be recognised and affirmed by the professional.

Issues for the final stage

1. Revisiting the past and relating it to the future

This is a time for revisiting the past with the family to help them to see how far they have come, and how much progress their child has made. This may involve a light-hearted look at some of the early misconceptions e.g. remembering how mother was unable to leave her child in nursery, whilst now the child may be in a full-time placement and mother out at work. Or it may be appropriate to remember some of the sadness and tears and to feel satisfied that this pain has passed. It is useful at this point to discuss how pain can recur at other crisis points in the future such as starting school, or at secondary school age when the child does not go into mainstream like his/her peers. The children have usually made a good deal of progress in these first two years and it is good to recall with parents how they feared that their, now lively, toddler would never walk, or that they would never resolve behaviour problems in a child who is now quite manageable.

2. Resolving last minute queries

Two or three visits before the final session, it is advisable to ask the parents to compile a list of outstanding queries or needs that may need to be resolved. e.g. they may require that their child is offered a full-time rather than a part-time placement, or they may decide that they wish to apply for a grant for a holiday or piece of equipment. Or indeed, they may wish to talk over some aspect of their child's development. The professional can then make every effort to help the parents with these queries, or give them the knowledge of how to seek help. Indeed, it is essential that the parents are carefully handed over to other key professionals more relevant to their new stage of development, e.g. class teacher or educational psychologist for the child's school.

3. Looking to the future

Often at this stage, the parents are able to tolerate and even enjoy the idea of their child's independence. However, they may still need to talk through with the trusted professional any residual feelings of guilt about wanting to pursue their own activities or to discuss anxieties and fears about the child's future. Again it is important to give the parents positive feelings about meeting their own needs, or about viewing the child's future in as balanced a way as possible. That is, being positive and realistic rather than falsely optimistic. All in all, there will be fresh goals to set and the professional can give the encouragement the parents need to move into the future with their child.

4. Handling the ending of the professional/client relationship

The emotional content of this ending phase cannot be overlooked. All through the relationship with the family, the professional will have been mindful of the need to work at the family's pace and following the agenda set by the family unit. This is equally important as the relationship draws to a close. Since the birth of their child with a disability, parents will have felt that control over their world is completely out of their hands, therefore, it is essential that they are given some control over how this phase in their life is ended.

Some of the grief the parents have felt about the loss of the dreamed-of normal child, and other losses they have felt in these early years, may be resurrected at the impending loss of the contact with this professional who has shared so much with the family. Consequently, it is not unusual for parents to 'panic' and even regress a little in an unconscious attempt to keep the professional in their life. The professional too has to avoid the temptation to hang on to clients s/he has come to view with respect and affection. Hence, these fears and hesitations must be discussed openly and honestly even with the professional sharing his or her own feelings about saying goodbye to the family; this helps to validate and normalise feelings of loss.

5. End on a positive note

If the case is closed slowly, carefully and sensitively, this stage can be used to emphasize the healthy functioning of the family, its wholeness and its new equilibrium. It will be clear to family and professionals alike that this is not the end of the story for the child with a disability nor his/her parents, but the working through of the grief and adjustment process has given the strength and skills to cope with the future. Life with a special needs child is a marathon run, not a sprint!

There will, of course, be families who cannot be helped towards this healthy conclusion. Some will have refused help very early on, or will willingly work with visiting professionals but are so heavily defended that the nature of involvement is only superficial. It is hard to measure the benefits of offering such an approach which sometimes may not bear fruit for many years but will at least be laying a foundation stone for other professionals in the future to build on.

Six

The needs of the child

IN EARLIER chapters we have stressed the prime importance of working with the disabled child's family, particularly with the emotional and the practical needs of the parents. However, we must not fall into the trap of a narrow approach that ignores the special needs of the child.

Parents usually seek a diagnostic label to help identify these special needs. They will also usually be concerned to know how the child is developing. They may want help and advice on how best to teach their child, either by asking for programmes or suggestions, or by requiring a nursery place that will offer the child specialist help, or the opportunity to mix with other children.

Sometimes, it is the professional who is concerned about the child, noting for example that he is not encouraged to play or to talk, or do things by himself. It is important then for work to be done to remedy this situation. The professional may also be asked for advice on the child's behaviour if this is an area of concern.

Identifying needs: The process of diagnosis

Attaching a diagnostic label to a child is of utmost importance to most parents, because they feel that then they are able to understand better both the cause and the consequences of the disabilities. It is true that diagnostic labels can be helpful for the child's present and future management. For instance, we know that Down Syndrome children tend to put on weight and therefore it is better to start a healthy low calorie diet early on, or that some syndromes always imply intellectual impairment and that parents need to come to terms with this aspect.

Once the diagnosis is made, it will be useful for the professional to contact a local or national society that deals with the particular syndrome or condition. Normally, they will provide pamphlets or booklets that describe the condition, the main needs of sufferers, resources available and advice to best help the child. Such groups also offer the possibility of contact with other parents whose children have the same type of disability. In the case of the most common conditions this can take the form of local support groups. In the case of rarer conditions there are national contact numbers available to enable parents to get in touch with others whose children have the same syndrome. Some parents, but not all, get comfort and support from sharing their questions and their concern with other parents.

When trying to define the child's needs and management strategies with the help of a diagnostic label, the following aspects should be kept in mind:

1. Each child, independent of his syndrome or condition, is a unique individual. Children who have the same condition will have some characteristics in common, but there also will be huge variations in their personality and skills, as is the case with any group of normal children.
2. Knowing the diagnostic label is useful for the more

frequent conditions such as Down Syndrome, or Spina Bifida, but there are about 900 syndromes identified and for many of these conditions there are so few sufferers that little is known about the needs of those children. There can even be genetic disorders which are characteristic of a single individual.
3. In some cases, the diagnostic label covers such a variety of cases that will not be very useful in determining needs. This is particularly the case of those children whose disability is due to brain damage. Terms such as spastic or cerebral palsy tell us very little apart from the cause of the disability.
4. Finally, in a high proportion of the cases, there is not a known diagnostic label for the child's disability. Parents have to adjust to the fact that they may never know the cause of their child's difficulties, and that they have no guidelines to understand the present or predict the future.

These four points give a clear indication of the necessity for an individual assessment for each child. Parents almost always see their son or daughter not as the sufferer from a condition, but as a particular individual. Professionals should take exactly the same view. From their knowledge of the child and the knowledge obtained from the parents, they should build a whole picture of the individual in order to determine the needs and the strategies to meet these needs.

Identifying needs:
The use of developmental charts

Developmental charts are scales that indicate at what age, on average, a population of 'normal' children will acquire a particular skill. Charts are divided in sections according to type of skill. For instance, a particular chart may have a scale for gross motor development, for fine motor development, for

THE NEEDS OF THE CHILD

use of language, understanding of language, self help skills, play and social developments. Different charts will use slightly different classifications, but they are all quite similar.

Developmental charts are useful because they can provide the following types of information:

1. An approximation of the general level of development of the child, as compared with the average population. e.g. Lucy is 4 years of age but her development is like that of a 2 year old child.
2. A comparison between different developmental areas. For instance, is the child delayed only in his ability to talk but not in his understanding of language? Is the child delayed in all areas, but particularly in social skills?
3. A good approximation of what skills the child is ready to acquire and therefore could be used as objectives for stimulation programmes.
4. A measure of the child's progress when the chart is filled in at different intervals.

An example will help to clarify what we have explained up to now. Look at the motor scale and the language expression scale printed overleaf. They are taken from the Hebden and Whyte Developmental Charts. They have been filled in for a child who we shall call Lorraine, who is 3 years of age. Lorraine's skills in fine motor development are around the two year to 30 month level, but she is more delayed in her use of language, in which she is functioning at the 10-13 month level. The rest of the charts (not shown) indicate that language comprehension is also at the 1 year old level while her gross motor, social play and self help skills are at the $2^1/_2$ year old level.

From these results we could say that:

1. Lorraine is delayed in all areas of her development, but the delay is only moderate with the exception of language.

Figure 1
Two Sections of the Development Progress Charts (Hebden and Whyte) filled in for Lorraine, age 3

Fine Motor Development

Item	Approx age	Item passed	Comments and observations
Picks up small objects with delicate pincer grasp	18 months	+	
Builds towers of three blocks after demonstration	18 months	+	
Can turn two/three pages of a book	18 months	+	
Able to pour water/sand from one cup to another	21 months	+	
Picks up objects neatly and quickly	24 months	+	
Removes wrapping from sweet	24 months	-	
Builds tower of six or seven blocks	24 months	+	
Unscrews 3" lid	24 months	-	

THE NEEDS OF THE CHILD

Figure 1 (Continued)
Two Sections of the Development Progress Charts (Hebden and Whyte) filled in for Lorraine, age 3

Use of Language

Item	Approx age	Item passed	Comments and observations
Can produce two clear words besides Mama, Dada	12 months	+	
When alone babbles continuously (words or parts of words may be recognisable)	13 months	-	
Able to repeat (imitate) one short word said continuously to him	13 months	+	
Can produce 3/4 clear words	14 months	-	
Talks at lengh (in jargon) to people/toys	14 months	-	
Can produce four or more clear words	15 months	-	
Vocalises with gesture to indicate required object	16/17 months	-	
Six or more clear words	17 months	-	
Nine or more clear words including names (brothers/sisters/name of Teddy)	18 months	+	

2. We should advice stimulation in all areas, but particularly in the areas of language skills.
3. In the area of language we could establish as possible targets the following: 'To shake head for "no" '; 'To imitate sounds made repetitively'. These are apparently next in children's normal development. Therefore they are not too easy and not too hard.

Developmental charts will *not* indicate the child's future intelligence, especially for the younger children under 3 years of age. They will indicate if there are delays and if they are moderate or severe. If they are severe they will usually predict a long term disability. But they can not predict future attainments, neither in a normal nor in a disabled population.

How developmental charts are used with parents

1. After one or two visits, the professional may decide to talk to the parents about developmental charts and ask them if they would like to use them. She can bring a few charts and ask the parents to look at them. If parents express an interest, they will be asked whether they have any preference. It is nice but not essential to give parents a choice of charts. Some professionals have a strong preference for one chart, and they may be unwilling to use others, or they may prefer a chart which is linked to a stimulation programme such as 'Portage'. The choice for parents should always be whether or not to fill in a chart. The timing of introducing parents to these instruments is important. If there is a strong process of denial, the parent could be very upset or could fill in the charts mainly in terms of wishful thinking rather than reality.
2. If the parents decide that they want to use a chart, the professional will usually fill one of the scales with the parents to illustrate the procedure. It is not necessary to

fill in the scale in all its range (0-5 years). Checking normally starts at approximate the level in which the child may be functioning and then it moves back until it is clear that the child has reached all the previous skills (7 to 10 consecutive pluses). Then items are checked forward, until it would appear that the child is not attaining any further skills (7-10 consecutive minus). If the parents feel confident that they can use the charts, they can be left with them to complete. Alternatively, parents and professional may prefer to complete the whole chart together.
3. Once the chart is completed, results are then discussed with the parents. The levels at which the child is functioning in different areas of the development are discussed. Normally, parents are not surprised by the results, but there are times, particularly when there is an element of denial, when the parents may be distressed. They may not express openly their disappointment, so it is always important to explore their feelings about the charts' results.
4. If the parents want some structured stimulation programmes based on objectives or targets, the professional and the parents discuss together what targets they want to choose among those that are about to emerge, as explained previously.
5. The charts can be reviewed regularly at a frequency agreed between professional and parents. In general, it is not convenient to have intervals of less than a month, as it could be disappointing not to observe any changes. If the charts are examined every two or three months, it is easier to find newly acquired skills, and the evidence of progress can be very rewarding. Some parents use charts regularly for a period and then they lose interest. Other parents look at them just once or twice a year. It is always important to go along with parental wishes.

Developmental charts can provide very valuable information about the child, but the results should never be interpreted in isolation. The context within which they are considered should always include the following factors:

- *physical problems*
  hearing or visual loss, motor difficulties, a heart condition that may cause tiredness, epileptic type fits etc.
- *the personality of the child*
  age, whether she is active or placid, shy or outgoing, affectionate or reserved, confident or unconfident.
- *the environment that surrounds the child*
  relation with parents and siblings, personality of father and mother and other significant carers, attendance to nursery, amount and type of stimulation that the child receives etc.

The debate on stimulation

All children need stimulation whether or not they have special needs.

To stimulate a child means providing her with a variety of experiences appropriate to her level of development. It means talking and listening to the child, giving her objects to play with (not necessarily toys), smiling, touching, letting her hear different sounds, and showing her affection.

Most parents provide adequate stimulation to their children, but sometimes stimulation is lacking because the parent is depressed, has not had adequate parenting herself or is too harassed and has no time for that child. Some parents stimulate too much, some others too little; in the middle there is a whole range of 'good enough' stimulation in which the type and degree of experiences offered to the child varies.

For many years, and during the 1970s and part of the 1980s, there was an assumption that children with special needs required stimulation on the following lines:

- the more parental involvement the better;
- the earlier the better;
- the more structured the better;
- the longer and more intensive the better.

Researchers then found out that the above assumptions were not necessarily true. If parents provided good and appropriate experiences to their child, it did not matter if they used programmes, or if the stimulation was shared with other adults, and there was no need to 'work' rigorously every day to improve the child's development.

This does not mean that if parents want help with structured programmes, this should not be provided. Some parents who have special needs children may feel de-skilled and unsure and if somebody helps them to define specific targets for their child to achieve, they may feel more confident. Also, for some parents who are not offering enough experiences, some clear guidelines may provide them with the impetus or the knowledge to help their child. However, it should be the parents' choice to decide how they want to help their child.

Many parents say 'I want to treat her as I treated the others' and this choice is fine and parents should be reassured that their child's development will not be impaired by carrying out their views. The notion that all parents should use intensive programmes has created a number of problems in some families:

- Some parents may spent so much time working with the child with special needs that the other siblings are neglected.

- Some parents keep active all the time and this begs the question, is this to keep their grief at bay? If so, would the constant activity for the child's benefit prevent a normal bereavement process in the parents, or even create unspoken resentment when the child does not respond in direct proportion to parental input?
- Some parents who were told that they had to carry out programmes, did not feel that this was their style or their wishes. If they implemented the programmes, they would do it unwillingly; if they did not, they felt guilty.

Keeping in mind the above, there is always a place for sensitive and specific advice for stimulation. The professional needs to be aware of the child's needs and the parents' wishes and ideally should be able to offer a variety of options, ranging from casual advice in answer to a parent's question, to the design of a structured programme to help the child's development.

What kind of advice can be provided for stimulation?

1. Using the development charts to establish the level of development of the child, and advising the parents to use toys and activities suitable for that age group.
2. Recommending or lending books about toys or activities for children with special needs or for ordinary children; providing children's books appropriate to the child's interests and development; giving leaflets which give general advice on how to stimulate children or which give suggestions on how to develop a certain area such as language or fine motor skills. The leaflets that are available from the societies that centre on specific conditions, often bring useful advice on strategies to help the child.
3. Helping the parents to define goals to be achieved using the developmental charts and then working out together some suggestions of activities to achieve these goals.

THE NEEDS OF THE CHILD

4. Support some parents in using programmes already designed which include activities to achieve certain goals. The most widely used of these programmes in the U.K. is the 'Portage Project', which was developed in the USA in 1972. This programme involves assigning to each family a home teacher who assesses the child using a specific developmental chart, and then, with the help of cards with activities, provides an individual prescription of target behaviours to be achieved each week. Parents teach these skills or behaviours until the home tutor returns, normally a week later, to check on the progress. The professional who is interested in following this approach can train in how to use it. There are Portage groups in various regions that provide training. Alternatively, if the parents are keen to use this approach, they can be referred to a local Portage team, if one is available.

There are also programmes for normal children that can be used with youngsters with special needs . For example, many health visitors have used the first parent visit project developed originally at Bristol University.

Dealing with behaviour problems

Children with special needs often present with behaviour difficulties. The reasons are varied:

- A slow development means that normal developmental stages last longer, and learning appropriate behaviour patterns may take a considerable time. The tantrums of the terrible two's in a normal child may last 12 or 18 months, but in a child with developmental delay the tantrums may last for many more years.
- Children with disabilities feel the frustration of not having skills that allow them to master the world. A speech difficulty will prevent communication, a motor problem will make it difficult to ride a tricycle or follow mother or

insert a peg in a hole. The frustration is naturally expressed in anger and tantrums.
- Certain conditions such as brain damage may, in some cases, involve a lack of inhibitions of behaviour, or sudden outbursts of anger.
- From the point of view of the family, parents may find it difficult to establish clear boundaries for their special child. Feelings like being sorry for the child, guilt or unresolved anger may prevent the parents from being firm and consistent. As a consequence, and as it is the case for all children who have this type of upbringing, the child will grow up spoilt and insecure.
- Finally, there may be problems in the bonding process between the parent and the child. Rejection may happen consciously or unconsciously due to a child who, because of her needs, is already demanding or unresponsive. Or it may be that the guilt of the parents get in the way of the attachment process. A child who feels rejection will be angry and demanding and will reinforce a vicious circle of rejection in her relationship with her parents or other members of the family.

How can the professional help?

When children present behaviour problems, it is normally recommended that the family implements a 'behaviour modification programme'. Basically, these methods imply:

- Identifying one or a few behaviours that are a problem for the parents.
- Record its incidence for one or two weeks.
- Start a system that ignores negative behaviours, and rewards or reinforces positive behaviour.
- Progress is recorded to assess if the programme is working.

For instance, for a child who has tantrums, the parent will

ignore the tantrums and will give the child stars or sweets if the child has no tantrums during an outing.

It is beyond the scope of this book to enter into a detailed analysis of this approach. There are some very good books and booklets available that can be consulted by the professional who needs to know more about this subject. Some of them are listed at the end of this book.

It is important, however, to be aware of the fact that behaviour modification programmes are normally of no use if the person who implements them is not fully committed. Normally, parents will need a lot of support to carry out a programme at the best of times. If there are deeper issues such as grief and anger, the behaviour programme will not be carried through until the distressing feelings are dealt with. In the meantime, if the child's behaviour is making the home situation unbearable, it would be indicated to recommend respite such as periods for the child at a nursery or with a child minder.

Expanding the child's environment

Bringing up a child with special needs is a long term project, and both the family and the child will benefit from sharing the task of the upbringing with other people. These may be professionals such as nursery nurses or teachers when the child attends a creche or a special or a mainstream nursery, or playgroup leaders if a child attends a playgroup. They can be professionals who provide regular therapy, such as physiotherapists or speech therapists, or extended family, grandparents, uncles and aunts, or close friends. In some local authorities there are various systems of respite such as specialist foster parents or child minders, and residential homes for short term care.

From the point of view of the parents, people sharing their child's upbringing not only provides much needed respite.

They also allow them to feel that they do not have full responsibility for their child's progress or lack of it. They do not need to assume the full burden of treatment, and they have the opportunity to talk about the child's problems and achievements with somebody who has the parents' objectives in mind. People who know the child well and who share the tasks of bringing her up, often are seen as friends of the family.

From the point of view of the child's needs, there are many advantages. As it is the case with a normal child, the disabled child needs to be exposed to a variety of experiences that will enrich his/her life. In some cases, they need special stimulation that only a professional can offer; in other cases just being with different adults gives them a different perspective of social interaction. Sharing with other children in a group is also a necessary learning situation, especially when sometimes children with disabilities can be over-protected, over-indulged and isolated.

It is also frequently the case that behaviour modification programmes and programmes to develop self-help skills are more easily implemented by people outside the immediate family. Children may respond better and be less manipulative with people who are not so emotionally involved as their parents.

In an ideal situation, parents would be offered a choice of alternatives so that they could decide what type of help and support they wanted for themselves and their child. It is important to realise that special needs children and their families are not an homogenous population, and it is therefore essential to individualise support in accordance with the family's needs and preferences.

Seven

The use of networks to offer a whole service to disabled children and their families

HAVING ESTABLISHED that neither the child with a disability nor his/her family functions in isolation, it is important to look to the wider community to help in the diagnostic process and in sustaining the child within the family. The professional must bear in mind that s/he is part of a network and that in order to give a family a comprehensive service she owes it to them to keep open channels of communication with the people in this network. Within this network the tasks for the keyworker/professional involved with the family are as follows:

1. To be aware of all significant figures in the child's life including the professionals involved.
2. To target all the relevant information available relating to the child and his condition, and carefully share it with the parents.

3. To be alert to the limits of one's own professional skills and know when, and to whom to refer.
4. To facilitate the parents' use of the network, encouraging them to feel confident enough to negotiate with other professionals and authority figures. If this process is successful, parents can develop mature relationships avoiding the extremes of hostility or over-dependence.

Note that the healthy use of networks can go wrong and the fault may not necessarily lie with the keyworker/professional nor with the parents. In a world of shrinking resources, negotiations with institutions can become difficult and authority figures obstructive.

These are some of the key agencies/resources that the child and family may need to be involved with, bearing in mind that the roles of professionals and their agencies vary from individual to individual, and from agency to agency. This list is an overview and not meant to be exhaustive:

Health
Paediatricians
Health Visitors
Health Authority
Community Physician in Child Health
Assessment Centres/Child Development Teams
Audiologist
Speech Therapist
Physiotherapist
Ophthalmic Services
Occupational Therapist

Education
Mainstream Nurseries
Special Nurseries
Mainstream Schools

Special Schools
Child Guidance Service
Educational Psychologist
Portage Service

Social Services
Social Services Departments
Family Support Centres
Respite Schemes
Young Carers Schemes

Voluntary Sector
The voluntary sector has a large part to play in providing support to the child and family, with specific expert knowledge and experience on offer in many cases. Some of the parent-led resources can provide a much-needed personal perspective that professionals may not be able to give. However, it must be borne in mind that new parents may not be ready for this type of intimate sharing of experiences.

Consider:
Specialist societies such as:
Downs Children Association
Mencap
Scope (Formerly the Spastics Society)
Autistic Society
Royal National Institute for the Blind
Royal National Institute for the Deaf

National voluntary organisations dealing with children generally such as:
Barnardos
Save the Children

Local groups such as:
Parents Groups
Toy Libraries.
Holiday Schemes

Other significant resources
Housing Departments
Social Security
Citizens Advice Bureaux
Library Services
Financial Help, provided through charitable organisations
Suitable Books and Leaflets, to enhance parents
  understanding of their situation

Specialist therapies

It is very important that when the keyworker/professional identifies profound distress in family situations, s/he seeks out skilled therapists or counsellors for this purpose. Sometimes families will refuse such help and this will pose a dilemma for the keyworker. There is no quick solution in these cases but it is essential that the family continues to accept the keyworker and to feel emotionally 'held' at whatever level. Meanwhile, that professional should seek out guidance and support with her own efforts and try to move the family slowly towards accepting more specific help.

Eight

Case studies

Linking theory to practice

OUR MODEL has evolved from our experiences in the field of traditional child guidance work including family counselling, child development problems, and grief counselling and psychotherapy, coupled with 15 years in the field of disability. During this 15 year period we have worked intensively with more than 100 families where a child has been born with, or diagnosed as having special needs. Most of these children had learning disabilities, some had multiple handicaps or sensory or physical disabilities. Our work has been carried out on the outskirts of Liverpool in a predominantly working class area.

Briefly what we have done during these 15 years is to visit families with very young children with disabilities, on a monthly basis for a period of one to three years. The sessions last for between one and one and a half hours and are complemented by linking the parents with support in the community. We also developed resources such as parents' groups and a toy library. Initially our approach was very child-centred in that we used developmental charts, stimulation programmes and behavioural interventions. The sessions tended to be of a prescriptive nature even though, from the beginning, we accepted the notion of 'parents as partners'. Because we were truly concerned about empowering parents we listened attentively to their expressed feelings and gradually became aware that there was a deeper issue that needed to be addressed—that of parental grief. In becoming aware of this we slowly changed our approach and we started to allow more time in the sessions for the expression and working through of feelings. To underpin and structure our developing practice we drew on the work of other authors working in the fields of disability and grief.

This chapter will attempt to bring alive some of the concepts covered in this book, by describing and discussing actual cases. The following studies are intended to illustrate the complex nature of some of the family situations which may be encountered by professionals in the course of their work. The accounts are not just intended to describe problems but to confirm and emphasise the need for good practice and make the case for an individual approach.

To begin on a positive and encouraging note, the first cases described are those of healthy, functional families. It is useful at this point to remind the reader that, as noted in the text, there is usually a better prognosis for restoration to healthy functioning if the family is healthy before the birth of the baby with special needs. As is normal practice, names and circumstances of the families have been altered to protect confidentiality.

CASE STUDIES

CASE 1. THE A FAMILY

Mr. and Mrs. A already had a 4 year old boy when Mrs. A gave birth to a child with physical disabilities and developmental delay. This second child, a daughter, was very ill, but the whole family responded well to the crisis. We first became involved at the request of the child's paediatrician who felt that Mr. and Mrs. A needed advice about nursery schooling, and general counselling.

In the beginning, Mrs. A was the main focus of our involvement, as her husband was at work and the older child in school. For a number of visits, this mother was exhibiting symptoms of denial, particularly concentrating on the girl's physical problems and refusing to acknowledge other aspects of her slow development. However, over a few months, as Mrs. A began to face up to the full impact of her daughter's condition, the tears began to flow. It was essential at this time that Mrs. A was allowed to express her grief whilst feeling psychologically held by the professionals.

During this period we came to know Mr. A and realised the strength of his relationship with his wife and commitment to his children. As is common, while the mother did the crying, father played the role of the 'strong' parent. Nonetheless, the situation evened out over the months as Mr. A began to open up about some of his own feelings, this was exacerbated by the loss of his job. This event in itself opened new doors for Mr. A who started work in the field of special needs.

Being sensitive parents, Mr. and Mrs. A were acutely aware of the effects that their daughter's arrival had had upon their older child. The boy expressed his needs through problems he was experiencing in school, but by helping the parents to be alert to possible deeper issues they were able to help him to discuss his mixed feelings about his sibling.

Mrs. A's extended family were also very involved and provided a support network for the A family. Mrs. A was still at work and her parents offered child-minding for the girl; unfortunately, it emerged that Mrs. A was often left feeling guilty and in their debt.

Mrs. A began to question her role within the extended family, and this triggered her individuation process and helped her to leave behind some of the roles she had, by now outgrown.

During these weeks of growth, Mr. and Mrs. A gradually began to accept their girl's condition and her place in the family. Mrs. A made some sense of what had happened to them through their belief that the child had been given to them by God to look after. Having reached this level of acceptance the parents felt able to address the child's special needs, exploring developmental issues and making plans for her education. For us, this involved putting the parents in touch with the community network of help starting with a local Day Nursery. Mr. and Mrs. A learned quickly and they began to contribute to other groups such as a local Portage group and the national society relevant to their daughter's condition.

After two and a half years of monthly visits, the A family had found a new equilibrium, and apparently each family member had experienced personal growth through their crisis. We were able to withdraw from the case when the girl began attending her special school and to hand over the care of her case to another educational psychologist.

CASE 2. THE B FAMILY

The girl in this case was already aged two when she was referred initially for assessment with a view to placement at a special school nursery. She was born with primary hydrocephaly, severe spasticity, and blindness; in addition it quickly became apparent that she was also severely retarded in her development.

In spite of the severity and multiplicity of the child's disabilities, she was surrounded by love and attention within her family. Indeed, she was making wonderful progress in terms of responsiveness and sociability. She was most particularly attached to Mrs. B who devoted all of her time to this child. This was probably the biggest issue to be dealt with in the early stages of our relationship with this family.

The girl's life was constantly under threat because of the serious nature of her condition, and she needed total care. Consequently four key tasks emerged:

1. Mrs. B needed to be helped to share the care of her child, firstly with her husband and then with nursery and respite carers.
2. Mr. B had to be given the confidence to participate actively in the practicalities of caring for his daughter.
3. The family's elder daughter, aged 6 years, needed to be brought into the frame more as she seemed to be too compliant and accepting of her role as the healthy, coping child. We felt that this was storing up problems for the future. The parents also identified the older child's need for some individual attention and 'fun' time.
4. Mrs. B required help to make space for herself and her marriage as her identity was clearly being subsumed by the disabled child.

The early months of our involvement were very busy but

fruitful. Mr. and Mrs. B were keen to use the opportunity to talk about their feelings, their hopes and fears. They seemed to reach a new understanding of their situation; whilst continuing to be devoted to their child with very special needs, they were also able to express ambivalent feelings. They also began to see their able-bodied daughter's needs in a new light and began to attend more carefully to those.

We, as professionals, were also required to attend to practical issues with the family. They needed a good deal of guidance and support about acquiring suitable equipment to make life easier for the whole family, and they needed encouragement to visit the appropriate educational provision and work towards letting the little one go.

Over the months the family found a new balance; Mr. B was doing much more caring for his disabled daughter while Mrs. B developed a life outside of the home. The older daughter even began to be healthily naughty! A place at a special nursery was found, the child began to attend school and thrive. Even when the inevitable illnesses attacked this vulnerable child, Mr. and Mrs. B did not lose heart and placed their trust in the other carers involved in their lives. All in all, in spite of the profound nature of the B child's disabilities, this whole family was enabled to lead a very full life.

After two years, we were pleased to see this family functioning in a very healthy way. They had grieved and adapted to the demands of their very disabled child, without sacrificing other family members. In fact, as we finished the visits, Mrs. B had started a part-time job and the couple were considering respite care for their child in order to spend quality time with the older daughter.

CASE STUDIES

These first two cases are of course the best case scenarios, wherein the parents have not only adapted to the birth of their child with special needs but have entered a period of growth. There have been many such cases over the years where a very strong growth process can be seen. Others fall into a middle group where, with help and support, families can be enabled to travel through the adjustment process to restore equilibrium. However, these families do not necessary go on to grow and develop new lives. Sometimes further development can be hampered by external issues such as financial problems, or early hurts that somehow get in the way of growth.

CASE 3. THE C FAMILY

Mr. and Mrs. C lived in cramped accommodation when their son Dean was born. They were a very young couple with a chequered history; father and mother had been very hurt by severe family problems in their childhoods. Unfortunately, during Mrs. C's pregnancy she suffered an illness which affected her unborn child and Dean was born with a severe health problems and developmental delay. When the couple's health visitor referred the family to us, she was concerned that the young parents needed guidance and support with their child and that Mrs. C especially was very distressed by her child's disability.

Both parents were very committed to our involvement but the early sessions were marred by Dean's ill health and the need for major surgery. As a result, Mrs. C continued to deny Dean's developmental delay and hoped that he would 'catch up' after his physical problems were resolved. During this time we built a relationship of trust and support with Mr. and Mrs. C and focused on some of the important practical issues such as improving their housing situation, and discussing financial pressures.

Happily, Dean made a good recovery and he became more active and responsive, but it was clear that he was globally delayed in his development. Mrs. C had asked that we help her with stimulation programmes and together we completed a developmental chart and worked at some tasks appropriate to Dean's needs. This was a painful process for Mrs. C of course and her fears about her child's development were gradually aired. Although Mr. C was not always present during these home visits, his involvement during this time was invaluable. He had always been more accepting of his son's condition, and provided some very down-to-earth practical support for his wife. His loving acceptance of Dean helped his wife to move through the denial stage of grief, through the anger and the sorrow, towards her own acceptance of their child. It was important that we reflected back to Mr. C the importance of his contribution, bearing in mind how he had been undervalued in his past.

Interestingly, the periods of anger and sorrow opened up other wounds for Mrs. C who used one session to share with us her feelings in relation to early childhood experiences. Soon afterwards, Mrs. C was able to move on towards accepting that Dean required special help, and that it would be beneficial to them all if they could consider some part-time nursery provision for their child to help with his general stimulation. Mr. and Mrs. C built a very constructive relationship with the local nursery, Dean and his parents thrived on the extra support in this environment and Mrs. C's confidence began to flourish.

It is poignant that our closure of this case was hampered by the couple's housing difficulties; they continued to be inadequately housed in spite of our best efforts. However, Mrs. C. became pregnant again and this gave us more ammunition to press for rehousing. Thankfully, we were able to make our final visit to them in their new home.

CASE 4. THE D FAMILY

Paul D was nearly three years old when he was diagnosed as having marked learning difficulties. His developmental delay was of unknown origin, and Mrs. D. was upset and puzzled about her son's condition. It was especially difficult for the D family to accept Paul's problems as he seemed such a normal child with good social skills and excellent eye contact. Paul came to our notice only when he was referred for assessment with a view to a nursery school placement.

Although nursery school placement was at the top of the family's agenda, it became clear to the educational psychologist involved that there were other pressing issues to be addressed. Mrs. D was finding it very painful to face up to Paul's problems and so was unable to make decisions about the child's schooling. Hence it was important to offer Mr. and Mrs. D regular input to allow time to come to terms with what was happening to Paul.

At first, Mrs. D was very resistant to expressing her feelings about Paul, and Mr. D was usually at work - aloof from the home situation. In fact, although the visits were always pleasant, it felt like a long time before Mrs. D. began to discuss her sadness about Paul's disabilities, and even then these feelings were often expressed through comments attributed to members of the extended family e.g. about grandmother's disbelief, or grandfather's denial of the problems. This was certainly a case of working at the client's pace.

Slowly, but surely, Mrs. D began to explore Paul's special needs, working through developmental charts, discussing his behaviour problems and looking at special nursery placements. Although Mr. D was rarely around for our visits, it filtered through that he too was learning to accept Paul's problems, and that he was supporting his wife in this process of adjustment. It was also healthy that Mrs. D made time to discuss her other children not only in relationship to Paul, but in their own right.

Because of the delay in diagnosis, and the time and care taken to give the family the space to adapt to the Paul they had as opposed to the Paul they thought they had, we acted quickly when a nursery place was found. Maximum support was given to Mrs. D in the early stages, and efforts were made to build a firm bridge between school and home. This time spent appears to have paid off; Paul has since made the transition to full time special school, and the family has survived intact.

> Finally it is only fair and realistic to describe a case where a parent never resolved anger or expressed grief. This case is a study in denial when the pain of the truth is too much to bear

CASE 5. THE E FAMILY

Miss E was a single woman already marginalised in the community and as a consequence was very isolated. She formed a relationship with a married man and became pregnant. Her child, a girl called Julie was born with multiple disabilities, not least her physical disfigurements.

Miss E was discharged from hospital with her baby and she withdrew from the world. Her health visitor offered support and was so alarmed by Miss E and Julie's lonely lifestyle that she referred the case to us. We were equally concerned by the depth of distress in the situation. Miss E proved to be very difficult to help throughout our involvement as she denied all negative feelings about what had happened to her and claimed to fully accept her severely disabled child. However, she did want our help with an application to be rehoused from her tower block home and so we built our relationship upon this.

On one occasion Miss E did start to disclose her feelings and express her horror and confusion about her child and we hoped that this might open a door for us to help with these feelings. However, by the time we next visited, Miss E had withdrawn and we never again glimpsed the true feelings behind the facade of total acceptance.

As well as being concerned about Miss E's emotional well-being we were worried that Julie's need for stimulation were not being met because of mother's tendency to sit and cuddle her child at all times and because of her inward looking lifestyle. Even when the family was rehoused, they never went out; Julie was hidden away from the world with very little stimulation. Miss E and Julie rarely left their home except for occasional medical appointments.

Julie has a multitude of physical disabilities which necessitate the input of physiotherapists and occupational therapists, and with their help, Miss E was persuaded to take up a place in a special nursery for Julie. This seemed to be the only way to help the child, whilst being able to monitor the mother's well-being.

Two years later Miss E had another child, this time a healthy girl who was initially very accepted, although always taking second place to Julie. This child has been identified as having emotional difficulties since she started school. Miss E is very rejecting and disparaging of this second, healthy, daughter and we hypothesise that this child has become the container for all the mother's unexpressed anger and rejection originally meant for Julie.

> *This is one last case example which illustrates the need to quickly identify when our model of working is not appropriate and to then ensure that another, more fitting, method for helping is found.*

CASE 6. THE F FAMILY

Little Thomas was born to a teenaged single woman still living with her nuclear family in very crowded, chaotic conditions. Thomas was born with a congenital disability and his young mother seemed sad and bewildered. Although her family was supportive and loving towards her and her son, their handling of Thomas was often inappropriate and interfering. Miss F's family undermined any attempt to talk through Thomas's situation and moved between over-indulging him to ignoring him. They certainly could not give Miss F the space nor the privacy to grieve.

After a number of abortive attempts to see Miss F in her own home, it was clear that the visits were making everyone, including ourselves, feel uncomfortable. Miss F wanted help but was embarrassed to talk in front of her family, and the family made it obvious that they did not want to unearth any uncomfortable feelings.

Appointments were then made for Miss F and Thomas to come along to the Child Guidance Centre. Very early on, Miss F was saying how alone she felt with her worries about Thomas, and we felt that our monthly appointments were not enough to 'hold' her through this difficult time. We were aware that the local Family Centre was committed to offering places to children with special needs, and that it ran support groups for mothers. We had used these facilities before and felt confident that Miss F should be referred there for help.

CASE STUDIES

This proved very successful. The Family Centre staff were accustomed to using stimulation programmes and Thomas has thrived in this environment. Equally important, Miss F too has blossomed with the help and support of the people at the Centre. She has benefited from the structure and guidance of the staff, and enjoyed the chance to make peer group relationships with the other parents. She has found a way of meeting Thomas's and her own needs without alienating her family.

The case studies just described, serve to illustrate the complexity and diversity of the process of adjustment that families go through. This clearly indicates the need for a flexible response from the professionals. However, the common elements are also there; the grief and other powerful feelings, the difficulties in coping with the practical demands, and in most cases the gradual acceptance, the adaptation, and often the growth that follows the crisis.

You may ask, as we have 'Is outside support needed for this process of bereavement and adjustment? Are the resources within the family or with the help of friends not sufficient?' We believe that specialist help does facilitate the journey through major personal crises and the literature on bereavement and post traumatic stress tends to support this view. Moreover, having a disabled child is a rare occurrence, people are not normally aware of the facts that would help the understanding of the practical issues or the importance of a bereavement process. Families need to feel psychologically held and to be given information in order to cope with their pain and to adapt. This will help to prevent abnormal grief, will aid the adjustment process, and will give the child and the family the chance of the best possible outcome.

You may also ask if your professional orientation is appropriate for this type of work. The particular professional qualification of the helper is probably not important.

Murray Parkes in his book *Bereavement* states that 'Confidence in our ability to cope with the distress of others can be, and normally is, obtained by a process of attunement'. He adds 'By repeated exposure we gradually discover what we can do to alleviate distress and how much of it is inevitable and insurmountable'. If we agree with this statement, we can say that if people from the caring professions are interested in helping families with a child with a disability they will be able to do so by following some of the guidelines in this book and by learning to stay with and hold their clients' feelings of grief, until the journey through this particular bereavement is completed.

Appendix 1

A rough guide to the Children Act 1989 for professionals working with children with disabilities

What is the Act?

The purpose of the Children Act 1989 is to bring about real improvements in the law relating to children and their families. There is a continuing argument about whether the Act is going to be properly funded but it initiates significant reforms in four ways:

1. By promoting the notion of partnership between families of children in need and service providers, e.g. health, education, social services, housing departments.
2. By setting a new and perhaps higher threshold for compulsory state intervention in family life.
3. By correcting an hitherto unequal contest between families (parents, children, relatives) and the state (local authorities) where there is disagreement about compulsory state intervention. Also demands a higher state of preparedness in legal matters on the part of the local authorities.
4. By bringing together under one umbrella the statutory basis for services up to now offered by local authorities and health authorities, and which were derived from several different Acts (The Child Care Act 1980; the National Assistance Act 1948; NHS Act 1977). Part III of 1989 Act both spells out services that a local authority

APPENDIX 1. THE CHILDREN ACT 1989

must or may provide for children and families, and brings 'children in need' and 'children with disabilities' under one statute.

What is a child in need?

- The category for 'children in need' is wide. It includes children with disabilities, neglected or abused children, children with developmental difficulties and children suffering social and emotional deprivation. NB It pointedly *excludes* the young offender.

- The major role of the local authority is to *facilitate* the care and upbringing of children in need by their families.

- According to the Act a child is in need if:

  he is unlikely to achieve or maintain, or to have the opportunity of achieving or maintaining, a reasonable standard of health or development without the provision for him of services by a local authority under this part; his health of development is likely to be significantly impaired; or further impaired, without the provision for him of such services; or he is disabled (Section 17[10]).

- The provisions are intended to enable local authorities to support family life, although they may, in certain circumstances, charge for a service.

- The 1989 Act marks an improvement over Section 1 of the Child Care Act 1980 in that it sets out some of the specific services which can be, or must be, offered to children in need and their families. But there are only two absolute duties:

  1. to publish information about services provided;
  2. to open and maintain a register of disabled children.

Provision for disabled children

- Every local authority must open and maintain a register of disabled children in their area, which may be kept by means of a computer. It would seem that this should be a voluntary register so that a child should only be registered with the agreement of a parent. (There would seem to be a good case for a common register and a clear indication of the purpose to which it would be put).

- Authorities are required to provide services for disabled children which are designed to minimise the effects of their disabilities and to give them the opportunity to lead lives that are as normal as possible, e.g. the assessment of needs for the purpose of the Children Act 1989 may be undertaken at the same time as an assessment under the Chronically Sick and Disabled Act 1970, or 1993 Education Act.

- Local Authorities should promote the upbringing of children by their families using a variety of family support mechanisms, e.g. advice and counselling, home help, assistance in travelling to use services, holidays, and, in exceptional circumstances, cash. The provision of family centres is also required by the Act.
  NB. All Services (except advice and counselling) are to be means-tested except for those families on income support or family credit.

- Section 27 requires that when the Social Services Department seeks the assistance of the Housing or Education Authority these bodies must assist if that help is compatible with their statutory duties and does not unduly prejudice the discharge of their functions.

Other key concepts

1. *Parental responsibility*

   The Act does not talk about 'rights' in relation to children but about responsibilities:

   - Assumes that bringing up children is the responsibility of parents and that it is the state's job to ASSIST rather than INTERVENE

   - Part I of the Act deals broadly with the allocation of parental responsibility e.g. There may be joint parental responsibility; a person who has parental responsibility may not surrender it, nor transfer any part of it, 'but may arrange for some or all of it to be met by one or more persons acting on his behalf (Section 2[9]) i.e. responsibility can be delegated to schools or holiday organisations.

   - If necessary, parental responsibility can be conferred through Court Order. e.g. Residence Order or Care Order.

2. *Welfare of the child is paramount*

   The Court has its own checklist to guide its decisions about the child's welfare. It covers:

   a) ascertainable wishes and feelings of the child;
   b) physical, emotional and educational needs;
   c) age, sex, background;
   d) likely effect of any change.
   e) any harm which the child has suffered or is at risk of suffering;
   f) the capabilities of the parents;
   g) the range of powers available to the court in the proceedings in question.

3. *Significant harm*

   The phrase 'significant harm' appears particularly in

connection with the EMERGENCY PROTECTION ORDER, CHILD ASSESSMENT ORDER, and CARE PROCEEDINGS. It represents a move towards a higher threshold for compulsory state intervention in family life:

- What does the term 'significant harm' mean?
  The Act defines harm as 'ill treatment or the impairment of health or development'. This can include sexual abuse and forms of ill treatment which are not physical. *The word 'significant' does not necessarily mean substantial.*

4. *Contact*
   Contact is deemed to be a fundament part of parental responsibility. 'Every local authority shall take such steps as are reasonably practicable, where any child within their area who is in need and whom they are not looking after, is living apart from his family:

   a) to enable him to live with his family; or
   b) to promote contact between him and his family, if, in their opinion, it is necessary to do so in order to safeguard or promote his welfare' (Schedule 2[10]).

5. *Judicial non-interference*
   The law should interfere as little as possible in family life. Any order will be judged relatively; it must be seen to produce something better for the child than any of the alternative arrangements available.

Appendix 2

Code of Practice on the identification and assessment of special educational needs: A brief guideline with special reference to preschool children

What is the Code of Practice?
In 1993 Parliament approved a new Education Act. In one of its sections this new act sets responsibilities to the governing bodies of schools in relation to all children with special educational needs. These are children who have difficulties in learning as competently as the majority of the other pupils and therefore are in need of extra help.

The Code of Practice was written to give practical guidance to Local Authorities, governors and teachers so that they can meet the responsibilities set in the 1993 Education Act towards special needs children. The Code has been approved by Parliament and started to be implemented in September 1994. Its recommendations are not legally binding, but if the Local Authority of the school decides not to implement them they have to prove that the system that they have in place is at least as adequate as the one suggested in the Code.

How does a child with special needs benefit from the recommendations of the Code?
- It requires early identification and help for children who present with difficulties in school.

- It encourages a careful professional assessment of the child involving a multidisciplinary assessment if appropriate.

- It considers the parental views at all stages of the process and the provisions of special tribunals to examine parental complaints.

- It requires that the child receives an education appropriate to his/her needs.

- It guarantees regular monitoring of the appropriateness of the educational provision.

- It indicates set times for reviews, assessments and statements so there should not be undue delays in implementing the recommendations.

What are the main points of the Code?

1. *Early identification*
The Code gives school the responsibility to identify as early as possible any child who has special educational needs whether they are minor or severe, whether they are temporary or more permanent.

2. *A staged model*
Under previous legislation, unless a child had a statement, the Local Education Authority or the school were not legally obliged to do anything. The new 1993 act recognises that there is a continuum in terms of special educational needs. A child may have a minor problem that requires some particular help, or may have various degrees of difficulties including severe disabilities. In this act *all* children with special needs must have these needs recognised and addressed.

APPENDIX 2. CODE OF PRACTICE

To implement this principle the code sets a five stage model.

Stage 1   The class teacher identifies a pupil who is having problems, informs the parents and sets special educational strategies to help the child.

Stage 2   If the teacher and the parents think that the child continues having problems, they ask the school's special needs coordinator to become involved. Every school has to nominate a teacher to advise on children with special needs.

In partnership with the parents and the class teacher, the special needs coordinator draws up an Individual Educational Plan (IEP) that sets specific goals for the child to achieve and indicates programmes and special resources needed to reach the objectives. These IEP's have to be regularly monitored and reviewed at all stages.

Stage 3   If insufficient progress is achieved, the school will ask for the advice of an outside specialist. For example, an Educational Psychologist, a teacher who specialises in learning or behavioural difficulties, an adviser on children with sensory impairment etc. Following the advice, new IEP's are drawn.

Stage 4   If the needs of the child are still not being met satisfactorily, the headteacher will write to the Local Education Authority asking them to carry out a formal assessment of the child's educational needs to assess whether a Statement of Special Educational Needs is required. The LEA then decides whether there is sufficient information to do a full assessment. If this is the case, they will ask the opinion of relevant professionals, of the parents and the pupil if s/he is old or mature enough, and of the teachers.

Stage 5   If the LEA considers that the child's needs are very significant and need resources that the school can not normally provide, they will write a *Statement of Special Educational Needs*. The results of the statement may imply that the child stays in a mainstream school with special support or that a special school is recommended. In the latter case, the parents are given a choice of suitable special schools.

3. *Parental involvement*
The parents' opinions are of utmost importance. They are informed and consulted at every stage and are given mechanisms to appeal if they are not in agreement with any decision.

4. *Monitoring*
The child's progress is reviewed regularly. The intervals for this monitoring process are defined in the code.

What are the procedures for under fives?
As many children under five years of age are not yet in school, the above recommendations in terms of school involvement obviously do not apply. However the four principles described above are still applicable.

Collaboration among agencies
The code stresses the need for interdisciplinary collaboration. The Health Authorities or Health Trusts, the LEA, the Social Services Department and Voluntary Agencies should all work together to provide advice and resources to help children with special educational needs. In the case of preschool children

APPENDIX 2. CODE OF PRACTICE

the need refers to the likelihood that the child will present special difficulties at the age when s/he will attend school.

The LEA's obligation to inform about local procedures
The LEAs should provide all the agencies working with children under five with information about the local procedures to identify children with special educational needs. The information may include record forms indicating causes for concern, the observations that have shown that the child has difficulties, confirmation that the parents have been informed and the views of any relevant people.

Identifying agencies' obligation to gather information and to try different strategies to help the child
If any agency identifies a child as possibly having special needs, they have to discuss this information with the parents. Then, with parental consent, they should also get further information from the Health Authority or Health Trusts. They may also consult with other professionals that could advise on how to best help the child.

When to inform the LEA
The LEA will be informed if the child's difficulties are still causing concern. Previously, this should be discussed with the parents, whose views should be listened to and who should be made aware of any voluntary agency that could offer support to them.

Criteria for statutory assessment
Once the LEA is informed, it may decide to ask for a formal assessment of special needs (as in stage 4 for school children) or the child may be informally referred for further diagnosis or clarification of the difficulties. The referring agency needs to provide evidence that it has sought sufficient advice and has to inform of what has been tried already to help the child.

The person whom the LEA contacts to clarify the needs could be for instance an educational psychologist or a pre-school adviser or a child development team. In some instances the advice is all that is required at this point. In other cases it may be clear that a statutory assessment is required.

The statement for preschool children
The statutory assessment may lead to a Statement, which for children between 2 and 5 has the same format as those for older children. The statement will be issued if the child's needs are very complex and if extra resources are necessary to meet these needs. Extra resources are those that cannot be accessed unless the child has a Statement. This support may take the form of a home based programme, the use of special professionals, such as clinical psychologists or specialist teachers, or a nursery class in a special or a mainstream school. The LEA should have available a list of all the provisions available for special needs children.

Children under 2
Children under 2 years will seldom have a Statement. They will have a Statutory assessment only if there is a request from the parents or if the needs are too complex and can only be met if the child has a Statement. This Statement does not need to have the same format as that of older children.

SOME MORE INFORMATION
ABOUT STATEMENTS

The statement is a document that sets out the child's needs and all the special help that s/he should have. This may include additional equipment, extra staff time, small groups, specialists' help etc.

It is assumed that only a minority of children with special needs will have a statement. This will only be drawn for children whose needs are more severe and complex and who need resources which are not normally available in their school or their community. A statement does not necessarily imply that the child will attend a special school as it may indicate that the needs of the child may be met in mainstream education with additional support. Some statements last for all the period of the child's education, others are only temporary. All statements are reviewed annually.

Appendix 3

Useful books and other resources

On information about different conditions

Contact a Family Directory (CAF). Contact a Family, 1991.
An invaluable manual with a list of almost 900 syndromes and conditions describing their characteristics, contact groups and publications.
Address: 170 Tottenham Court Road, London W1P OHA.

Brudenell, P., *The Other Side of Profound Handicap*. Macmillan, 1986.
A good description of different syndromes and conditions.

On working with parents

Pugh, G., *Parents as Partners*. National Children's Bureau, 1981.
A pioneer book describing different programmes involving parents of handicapped children.

Sanctuary, G., *After I'm Gone, What Will Happen to My Handicapped Child*. Souvenir Press, 2nd Edition, 1991.
A useful book to provide practical advise to parents who are concerned about what will happen to their son or daughter after their death.

McCormack, M., *Special Children, Special Needs*. Thorsons, 1992.
Families talk about the problems and the events that they have experienced throughout the handicapped child's life.

On bereavement in general

Worden, W., *Grief Counselling and Grief Therapy. A Handbook for the Mental Health Practitioner*. Routledge, 2nd Edition, 1991.
An excellent book on bereavement discussing the tasks of mourning, grief, counselling and the different types of losses.

Murray-Parkes, C., *Bereavement: Studies of Grief in Adult Life*. Penguin, 1972.
This was the first book to introduce modern ideas of bereavement and the fact that it can develop because of death as well as other types of losses.

On methods to help with behaviour problems

Carr, J., *On Helping Your Handicapped Child: A Step-By-Step Guide to Everyday Problems*. Penguin, 1980.
It provides with good and simple advice on how to help the handicapped child to develop self help skills and to improve behaviour.

Herbert, M., *Banishing 'Bad' Behaviour: A Trouble-Shooting Approach for Practitioners Working With Childhood Behaviour Problems*. IMPACT Desktop Publications, 1993.
A clear practical manual to be used by professionals working with parents whose children present with behaviour problems.

Pollack, G. & Johnson, C., *My Child Has Temper Tantrums,. What Can I Do About It?* Knowsley Borough Council, 1995.
An illustrated booklet with suggestions for parents who want to understand and deal with tantrums.

On how to help with the development of the child

Lear, R., *Play Helps, Toys and Activities for Children With Special Needs.* Butterworth and Heineman, 3rd Edition, 1993.
Suggestions of games, materials and activities to help handicapped children develop sight, hearing, smell, touch and taste.

Cameron, R.J. & White, M., *Portage: Early Education Programme.* NFER Nelson.
A checklist, a box of activity cards and a manual that can help to implement a structured stimulation programme.

Jeffrey, D. & McConkey, R., *Let Me Speak.* Souvenir Press, 1991.
A book for parents giving suggestions of activities to stimulate language skills.

Riddick, B., *Toys and Play for the Handicapped Child.* Chapman and Hall, 1991.
A book that shows toys and games that can help the development of the disabled child.

On counselling in general

O'Farrell, U., *First Steps in Counselling.* Veritas Publications. 1988.
Street, E., *Counselling for Family Problems.* Sage Publications, 1994.
These two books offer a good basic guide to counselling and would expand some of the ideas suggested in the present book.

APPENDIX 3. BOOKS AND OTHER RESOURCES

Books for the child or the siblings.

Franklin Watts' Series of books for children who have a disability, 96-98 Leonard Street, London EC2.
Picture books in which children tell their story. There are books on asthma, blindness, Downs Syndrome, epilepsy, cerebral palsy, spina bifida, deafness etc.

Laird, E., *Red Sky in the Morning*, Heinemann, 1988.
The story of an adolescent girl with a baby brother who has a disability.

Meyer, D., *Living with a Brother or Sister With Special Needs*. University of Washington Press, 1985.

On the Code of Practice.

Special Educational Needs: A Guide for Parents. Department for Education, 1994.
A booklet that explains the Code of Practice to parents.

On the Children Act

An Introduction to the Children Act, 1989. HMSO, 1989.

On further resources

Mencap publishes an excellent catalogue that lists and briefly describes books dealing with all aspects of disability. Address: 123 Golden Lane, London EC1 0RT